Co

Party Time

SEND INVITATION CARDS DECORATED WITH A PUMPKIN WITCH

THE MINIATURE BOOK OF

Halloween

a Salamander book
Published by Salamander Books Limited
LONDON • NEW YORK

A SALAMANDER BOOK

Published by Salamander Books Ltd
129-137 York Way,
London N7 9LG
United Kingdom

ISBN 0 86101 699 8

Distributed in the United Kingdom by Hodder and Stoughton Services
PO Box 6, Mill Road
Dunton Green, Sevenoaks
Kent TN13 2YA

CREDITS
All projects created by Lyn Orton except for pages 8 and 9 by Annette Claxton, pages 12, 13, 40 and 41 by Cheryl Owen and pages 20, 21, 26, 27, 32 and 33 by Suzie Major.

EDITOR: *Alison Leach*
PHOTOGRAPHERS: *all photography including cover by Jon Stewart, assisted by Sandra Labell, except for the following: pages 8, 9, 40 and 41 by Steve Tanner and pages 20, 21, 26, 27, 32 and 33 by Terry Dilliway*
DESIGNER: *Louise Bruce*
STYLIST (COVER): *Barbara Stewart*
ILLUSTRATOR: *Pauline Bayne*
Typesetter: *SX Composing Ltd*
COLOUR SEPARATION: *Regent Publishing Services*
Printed in Belgium by Proost International Book Production

1 Cut a piece of thin red card 22 × 16cm (8½ × 6¼in). Score and fold 11cm (4¼in). Make patterns in white card for witch's hat and pumpkin head. Cut out a witch's hat from black paper or card. Cut out a pumpkin head from orange paper or card. Cut out diamond and triangular shapes for features as shown.

2 Lay head and hat patterns on red card and mark positions with a sharp pencil. Glue pieces in place.

3 Add multi-coloured sequin stars and moons, using glue, holding them in place for a moment while glue dries. Tweezers make it easier to handle the sequin shapes.

Ring O' Witches

HANG THIS RING ON THE DOOR TO MAKE YOUR GUESTS SHUDDER

1 Cut 1 metre (39in) of 225g (8oz) polyester wadding (batting) into 10cm (4in) wide strips. Use to bind a florist's double metal ring, 30cm (12in) in diameter, tucking the ends in firmly. Then bind with strips of 50g (2oz) polyester wadding. Repeat this step with black fabric to cover wadding, then with black net.

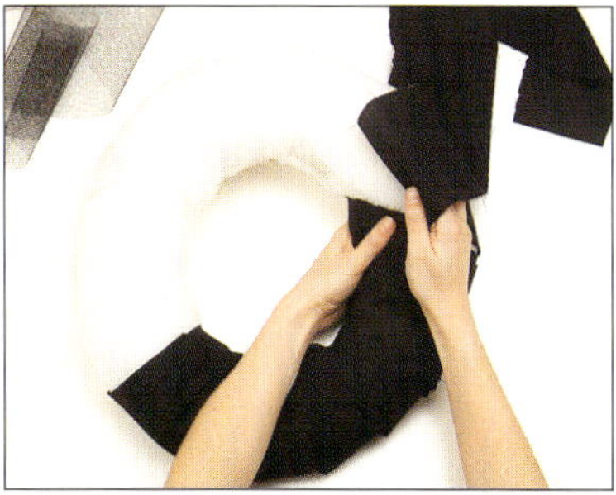

2 It is easier to decorate the 5cm (2in) acrylic pompons after they have been sewn onto the padded ring, alternating green and white. To make faces, decorate each pompon with joggle eyes, 5mm (¼in) green acrylic pompons, strands of hair and red felt mouths.

3 Make patterns for witch's hat and cut out in thin black card. Apply glue in a thin line on opposite sides of crown. Twist to overlap and join when glue is tacky. Glue crown to brim and then stick onto pompons. Wrap strips of black net around ring and knot on outside. Make a net loop for hanging ring on door.

Jack O' Lantern

USE A LARGE RIPE PUMPKIN TO MAKE THIS JOLLY JACK O'LANTERN

1 Using a very sharp knife, cut a slice off the top of a pumpkin. Scoop out flesh and seeds, leaving about 2.5cm (1in) rind. Use flesh to make a pumpkin pie. Wash and dry seeds, scatter over a baking sheet and sprinkle with salt. Bake in a moderately slow oven until dry and crunchy.

2 Mark eyes, nose and mouth on front of pumpkin with a black felt pen. Cut carefully around lines, then push features out from inside. Rinse inside of pumpkin and dry thoroughly with absorbent kitchen paper.

3 Put a couple of nightlights inside, light them and replace top of pumpkin. Place on a wide windowsill to frighten away any spooks. Make sure curtains are safely drawn back.

Pussy Cat Mask

A CAT'S HEAD MAKES AN IDEAL SHAPE FOR A HALLOWEEN MASK

1 Referring to photograph, make a pattern for mask in thin white card. Lay on a piece of black felt. Trace round outline with dressmaker's chalk and cut out. Then use pattern to cut out an identical shape from a piece of craft quality Vilene (interfacing). Cut out holes for eyes and pin felt and Vilene shapes together.

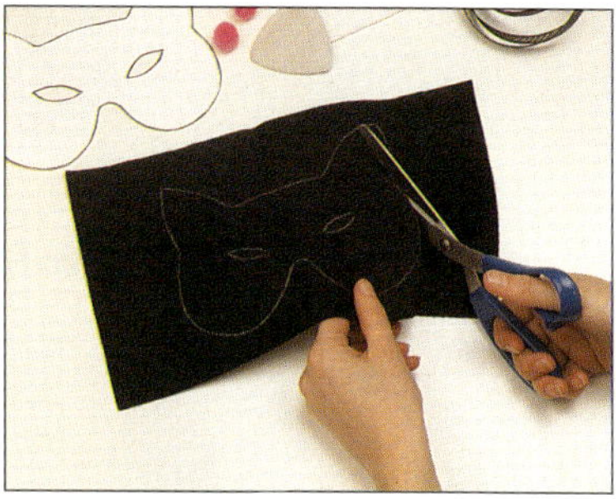

2 Join mask shapes together (there is no 'right' side to either felt or Vilene) with small running stitches about 5mm (¼in) from edge. Use a craft knife to neaten eye holes if necessary and outline with small running stitches.

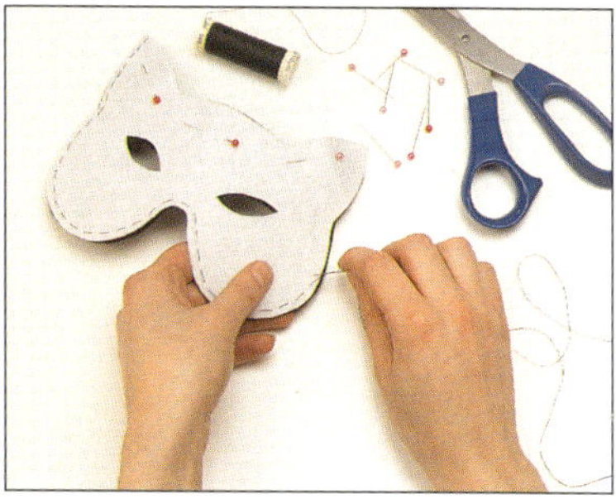

3 Glue or sew on whiskers and eyebrows, six 5mm (¼in) pink pompons for jowls and a 2cm (¾in) pink pompon for nose. Measure around your head and cut a length of 12mm (½in) wide black boning, allowing a 2cm (¾in) overlap. Pin overlap together, then stitch securely to centre of forehead on Vilene side of mask.

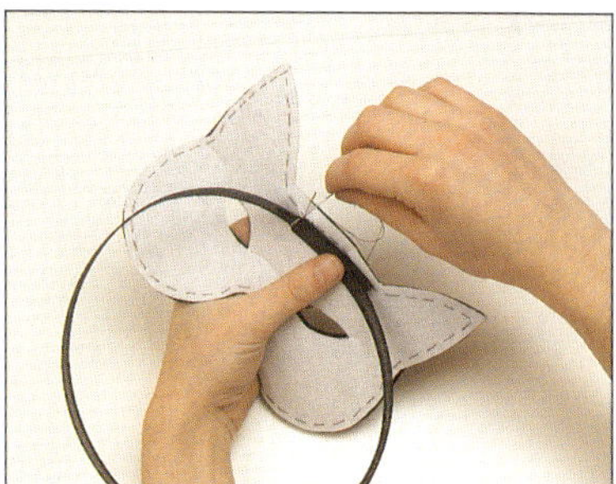

Horrible Hand

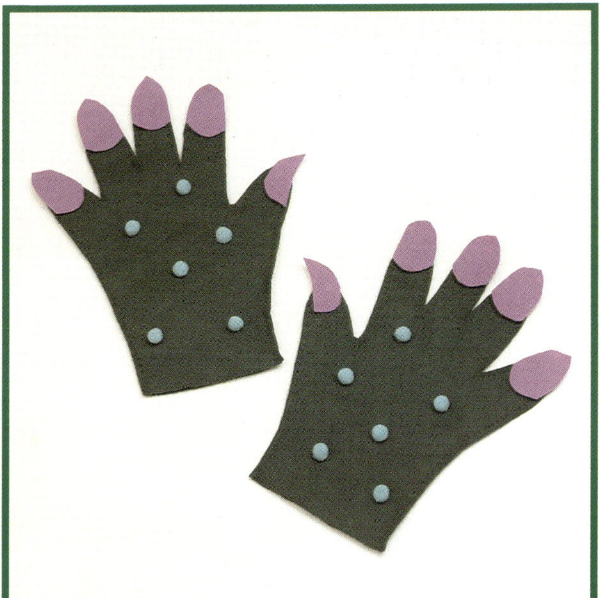

POINTED FINGERNAILS AND WARTS TO MAKE YOUR HAND GROTESQUE

1 Trace round one hand onto thin white card. Following outline, make a slightly larger spookier hand and cut out.

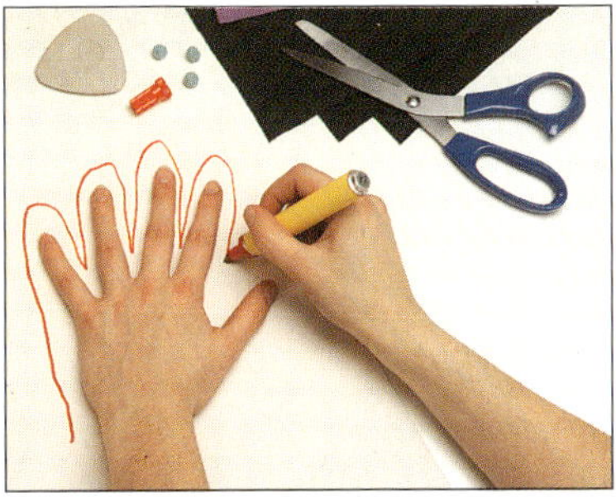

2 Lay hand pattern on two 30cm (12in) squares of green felt pinned together. Using dressmaker's chalk or a felt-tip pen, mark outline, then cut out carefully. Cut out and shape five long pointed fingernails in mauve felt.

3 Pin both hand shapes together and stitch about 3mm (⅛in) from edge. Attach fingernails with glue and stick a few 10mm (⅜in) diameter turquoise acrylic pompons over back to represent warts. Make a second 'glove' in same way to complete the spooky effect.

Boxy Paper Chains

TRADITIONAL PAPER CHAINS CAN BE MADE TO LOOK REALLY EERIE

1 Referring to photograph, make patterns for a frog, spider or skull in thin white card. Lay pattern on appropriately coloured card. Trace round outline with dressmaker's chalk or a felt-tip pen and cut out required number of shapes.

2 Choose main colour for chain and cut coloured card into 23cm (9in) lengths, 5cm (2in) wide. Form a ring with one length by applying glue to opposite sides of ends. Link a second ring to first as shown and continue until chain is completed to required length.

3 Hold chain firmly and fold alternate links horizontally and vertically to create a boxy effect. Decorate each front-facing link with either a frog shape with joggle eyes and black spots, a spider with joggle eyes, a skull marked with a black felt-tip pen, or your own design.

Wicked Witch

DECORATE A TRADITIONAL WITCH'S HAT WITH GOLD STARS AND MOONS

1 Take a large piece of black art paper, measuring 39.5 × 38cm (15½ × 15in). Mark a 1.5cm (½in) border at one end of longer side so that you have a 38cm (15in) square. Using chalk, string and drawing pin, draw an arc between other two corners as shown.

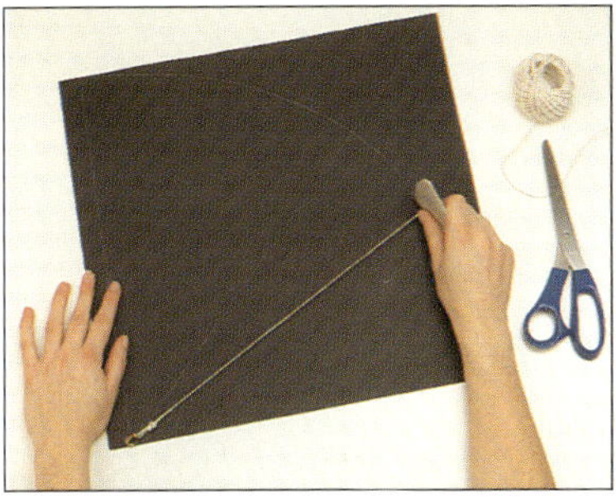

2 Cut along arc, spread glue on border and use this to join edges of cone together. Use cone to mark a circle on some black card. Draw another line around the first, about 5cm (2in) from it, then another just 2.5cm (1in) inside first line. Cut carefully along the inner and outer lines, then make triangular cuts on inside of brim.

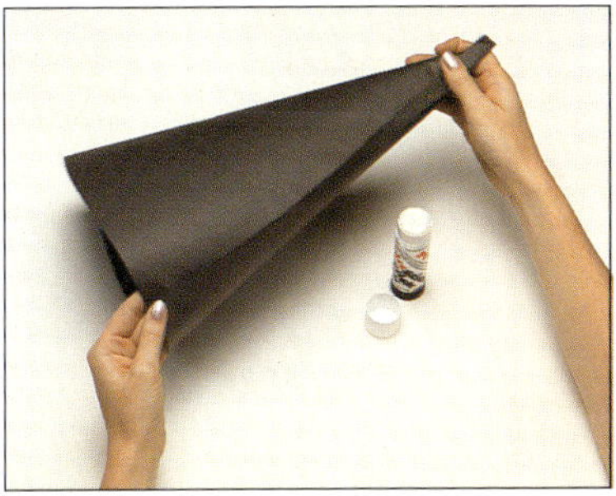

3 Bend triangular cuts upwards and glue them to inside of cone. Decorate hat with gold stars and moons cut from self-adhesive plastic.

Witch's Treasure

REMEMBER A WITCH NEEDS COSTUME JEWELLERY FOR A PARTY

1 Form a piece of black or red chenille pipe cleaner into a ring and attach a matching 5cm (2in) acrylic pompon with glue. Decorate black pompon with silver stars or red one with 5mm (¼in) black pompons. To make bracelet, form black chenille pipe cleaner into a ring, attach four pompons with glue and decorate with silver stars.

2 Form a piece of green chenille pipe cleaner into a ring and attach three 5cm (2in) green acrylic pompons with glue. Twist a length of green chenille pipe cleaner into a snake shape, securing one end around bracelet. Decorate snake with 5mm (¼in) green acrylic pompons and add a pair of joggle eyes, as shown.

3 Bend four black pipe cleaners. Glue onto 2.5cm (1in) black acrylic pompons. Tie a length of 3mm (⅛in) wide red satin ribbon in a bow, leaving 7.5cm (3in) to knot onto earring hook, and sew onto head of spider. To make frog earring, cut out shape in a double thickness of green felt, add joggle eyes and scraps of felt. Pin an earring hook in frog's head.

Grisly Glasses

FRIGHTEN YOUR FRIENDS BY WEARING THESE JOGGLE-EYES

1 Cut out two rough star shapes in red felt. Attach to two 3.5cm (1⅜in) diameter white acrylic pompons with glue. Stick a different sized joggle eye onto each red star.

2 Form two 2.5cm (1in) diameter rings from two 15cm (6in) pipe cleaners. Curve half a pipe cleaner and use to join rings.

3 Attach one end of a pipe cleaner to each ring and bend the other end to fit behind your ear. The glasses should rest on end of your nose. Glue decorated pompons in position so that joggle eyes are peering through frame.

Mysterious Masks

ADD GLAMOUR TO YOUR HALLOWEEN PARTY WITH THESE PRETTY MASKS

1 For a stunning party mask, buy a ready-moulded mask from a stationer's or toy shop. The half-mask shown here is coloured with oil stencil pencils. Start with the pink; apply a little to a piece of waxed paper, then pick it up on the stencil brush. Using a circular motion, cover about half the mask. Repeat with the blue, filling in the gaps to resemble eyeliner.

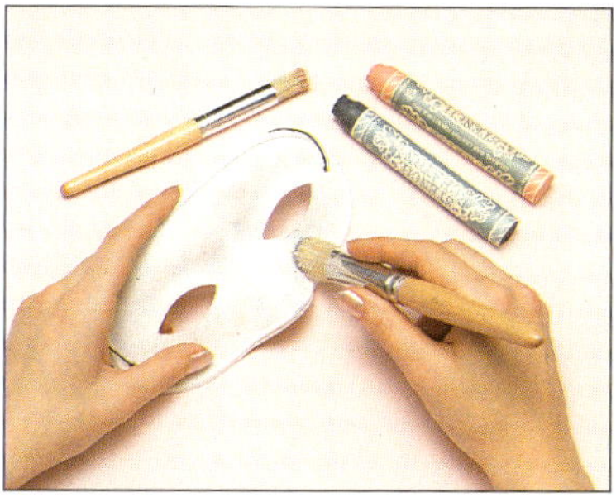

2 Next take a short length of lace and glue it to the back of the top half of the mask, down to where the elastic is attached. Glue some strands of curled gift wrap ribbon on either side. Lastly, glue some large sequins over the tops of the ribbons to hide the ends, and glue a larger sequin in the centre of the forehead.

3 For the black mask, first sew some silver tinsel wire around the edge and around the eyes. Sew on some pearl beads either side, then sew two or three grey or white feathers under the edges to create an owlish look.

Magic Kite

FLY A KITE AT HALLOWEEN
TO SCARE AWAY ALL
THE SPOOKS

1 Referring to photograph, copy large spook shape onto a 64 × 51cm (25 × 20in) sheet of dayglow card and then cut out. Make a pattern for smaller spooks, about 25cm (10in) high and 17cm (7in) across. Lay pattern on dayglow card, outline in pencil and cut out three shapes for tail. Punch a hole in top of each small spook. Glue joggle eyes in position.

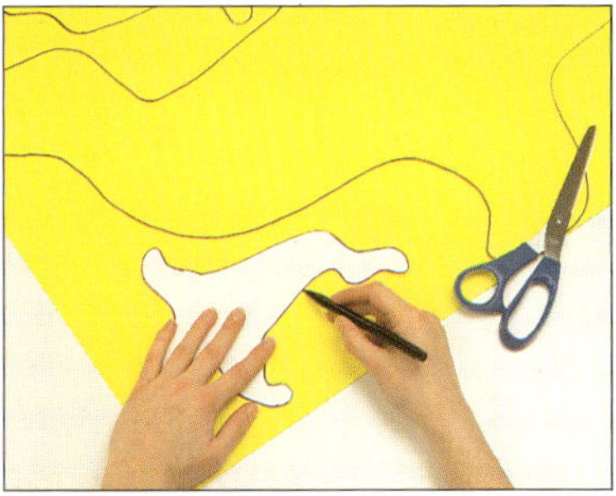

2 Using thick cotton thread, bind a 64cm (25in) length of 10mm (3/8in) wooden dowel very securely at right angles to a 82cm (31in) length, 23cm (9in) from one end. Slit open base of a black plastic rubbish (garbage) sack. Wrap crossed dowel in double thickness of plastic, securing with black plastic electrical tape on back of kite. Tape exposed points of dowel.

3 Attach one end of a 15 metre (50ft) length of black cord very securely to bound cross-piece. Thread smaller spooks equidistantly onto one end of 2 metre (6½ft) length of black cord, knotting cord between each one. Then knot cord onto base of kite and knot end of remaining cord on a curtain ring. Thread longer cord through curtain ring.

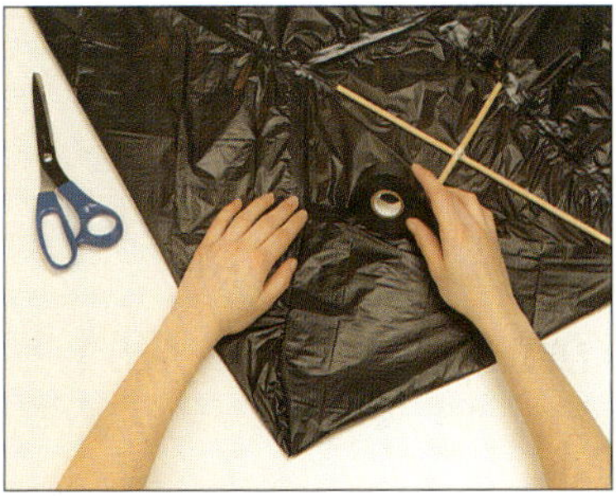

False Noses

WEAR GHOULISH NOSES LIKE THESE FOR SIMPLE AND ORIGINAL DISGUISES

1 Referring to photograph, make patterns for both nose shapes in thin white card. Use scraps of felt in different colours. Lay both patterns on a double thickness of felt. Trace outlines with dressmaker's chalk and cut out shapes.

2 Pin shapes and join together with small running stitches. Fill noses with small pieces of wadding (batting), pushing it in firmly. Cover top openings with matching felt sewn in position with small running stitches.

3 Colour some millinery elastic with ink or a chunky felt-tip pen to match chosen felt. Measure around your head and cut lengths of elastic for both noses. Overlap ends of elastic across covered top, as shown, and stitch securely; repeat with other nose. Decorate noses with acrylic pompons in contrasting colours for added impact.

Hanging Pumpkin

A QUILTED DECORATION TO BE USED AT HALLOWEEN YEAR AFTER YEAR

1 Cut out two orange satin shapes, following outline shown opposite. Place right sides together and sew around the edge, leaving flat part at bottom open. Turn shape right side out, tuck in a piece of medium-weight wadding and slipstitch gap together.

2 Mark quilting lines with tacking (basting) stitches using dark thread. Now machine quilt, using a small zigzag stitch and orange thread. If you haven't got a machine, a small backstitch will be fine. Remove tacking when you have finished.

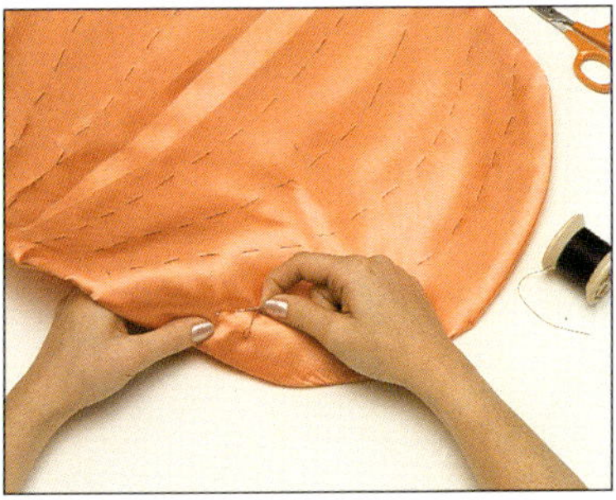

3 Cut out eyes, mouth and stem in black and green felt. Make loop from a piece of felt, about 13cm (5in) long, and attach under edge of stem. Preferably attach all felt pieces with a machined satin stitch using orange thread, rather than doing this by hand.

Magic Mascots

TRADITIONAL COMPANIONS OF A WITCH INCLUDE BATS AND CATS

1 Attach 5cm (2in) bulldog clips to one end of varying lengths of wooden dowel, 5mm (¼in) in diameter. Apply two coats of black gloss paint, hanging clips on hooks to allow paint to dry. Cut off tiny unpainted ends when dry.

2 Referring to photograph, make patterns for a bat, cat, snake and spook in thin white card. Lay patterns on suitably coloured card. Trace carefully round outlines with dressmaker's chalk or a felt-tip pen and cut out shapes.

3 Decorate snake with a large joggle eye and black self-adhesive spots of different sizes. Sprinkle glitter dust below bat's joggle eyes. Stick 2cm (¾in) green self-adhesive spots under cat's joggle eyes. Glue joggle eyes on spook. Glue painted dowels to backs of shapes.

Find Your Place

MAKE LITTLE WITCHES AS PLACE MARKERS FOR YOUR GUESTS

1 Referring to photograph, make patterns for brim and crown of hat, and dress in thin white card. Arrange patterns as shown on piece of thin black card about 30 × 20cm (12 × 8in) and cut out shapes. Using a craft knife, make an angled slit in front of dress as shown to hold place card.

2 Apply glue in a thin line on opposite sides of straight edges of dress and crown. Twist each piece to overlap and join when glue is tacky. Glue crown to brim of hat. Apply glue over part of crown and sprinkle with glitter dust. Leave to dry.

3 Decorate a 5cm (2in) white polystyrene ball with some black acrylic hair, joggle eyes, a pompon nose and hat. Glue neck edge of dress and press head lightly into position. Write guest's name on a 7.5 × 5cm (3 × 2in) white card and tuck into slit in front of dress.

Witch's Fare

MAKE THIS GRUESOME PIE THE CENTREPIECE OF A PARTY BUFFET

1 Cut out rough star shapes in red felt. Use glue to attach a star shape to six 5cm (2in) diameter white polystyrene balls. Add a joggle eye to centre of each star shape.

2 Line a 15cm (6in) diameter foil pie dish with a 30cm (12in) square of beige felt, gluing base and stitching side. Glue felt to top edge of pie dish and trim surplus felt to a rough circular shape to form a lip about 4cm (1½in) wide. Make a ring of felt about 4cm (1½in) wide to form a second lip and glue in place, easing lower lip as necessary to fit.

3 Fill pie dish with decorated polystyrene balls. Cut a 23cm (9in) scalloped circle of felt for lid and cut out a wedge-shaped piece. Pin, stitch or glue in position. Use remaining scraps of felt to make leaves to decorate top of pie.

Halloween Lantern

AN EERIE LANTERN TO CAST MYSTERIOUS SHADOWS ON THE WALLS

1 Cut a strip 50 × 22cm (20 × 8½in) of shiny black cardboard – the sort that is white on the back. Cut out a large and a small bat in thin white card. Use these patterns as templates to draw three bats on back of strip in top centre.

2 Cut out the bat shapes with a craft knife. Always use a cutting board to avoid damaging a work surface.

3 Overlap ends of strip and staple them together. To complete effect, place a few nightlights in a heatproof dish and lower lantern very carefully over it. Do not leave lantern unattended when it is lit.

Spooky Letters

CREATE SPECIAL WRITING PAPER FOR SENDING HALLOWEEN NOTES

1 Decorate a sheet of purple paper by overlapping two self-adhesive 15mm (⅝in) green spots, adding joggle eyes and drawing legs with a green felt-tipped pen. Decorate a sheet of grey paper with self-adhesive 15mm (⅝in) black spots, making a head with joggle eyes and a tiny red star for a mouth.

2 Decorate a sheet of green paper with self-adhesive 15mm (⅝in) black spots and turn into spiders by drawing legs with a black felt-tip pen. Decorate a sheet of black paper with self-adhesive 15mm (⅝in) green spots, with tiny curved strips cut from black spots for mouths and joggle eyes.

3 The two designs shown in this photograph are even quicker to make. Scatter self-adhesive blue stars over a sheet of red paper and matching envelope, or stick different sizes of black spots on a sheet of green paper.

Cast a Spell

WAVE A WAND AT MIDNIGHT
TO SHOW OFF YOUR
MAGIC POWER

1 Attach a 5cm (2in) bulldog clip to one end of a 45cm (18in) length of wooden dowel, 5mm (¼in) in diameter. Apply two coats of black gloss paint, hanging clip on a hook to allow paint to dry. Cut off tiny unpainted end when dry.

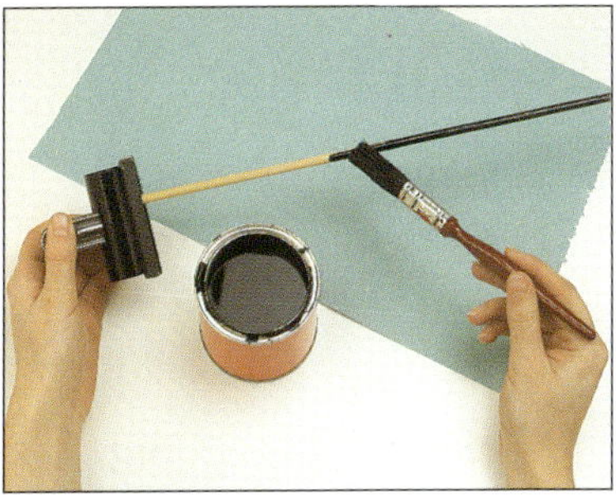

2 Referring to photograph, make patterns for a large and a small star in thin white card. Lay patterns on a 30cm (12in) square of thin black card. Trace round outlines with dressmaker's chalk and cut out.

3 Glue 10mm (⅜in) black acrylic pompons on points of small star as shown. Lay one end of painted dowel on large star and glue in position. Attach smaller star on top, as shown. Crescent-shaped pieces of yellow card may be used in same way to make a moon wand.